Kid's Library of Space Exploration

Missions to Mars

Space Exploration

Kid's Library of Space Exploration

Missions to Mars

Kim Etingoff

VILLAGE EARTH PRESS

Kid's Library of Space Exploration: Missions to Mars

Village Earth Press
Vestal, New York 13850
www.villageearthpress.com

First Printing
9 8 7 6 5 4 3 2 1

Series ISBN (paperback): 978-1-62524-444-4
ISBN (paperback): 978-1-62524-405-5
ebook ISBN: 978-1-62524-040-8

Library of Congress Control Number: 2014931525

Author: Etingoff, Kim.

Contents

First Missions to Mars

Humans have gone into space. We've circled the Earth. We've gone to the moon. But we haven't yet landed a person on Mars. Going to Mars could be the next big step in space exploration.

Scientists have already sent spacecraft there. They have even landed robots on the planet. We already know a lot about Mars, but there's a lot left to learn.

Way Back

People have known that Mars existed for a long time. That's because people have always been able to see it in the night sky. Mars is a small, red dot in the sky, which looks a little brighter and redder than a star.

Mars is often called the red planet, because it looks red from Earth. The rocks on the surface are red. We can see the red color even from very far away. Red reminded people of blood and war, so long ago, people named the planet Mars, after the Roman god of war.

For centuries, astronomers have followed Mars across the sky, making maps of where it was in different seasons. They also figured out how far away Mars was.

As soon as people invented the telescope, they used them to look at Mars. With telescopes, people could see mountains and canyons on Mars' *surface*. They saw big *craters*. They didn't see much evidence of life though.

People have wondered if there could be life on Mars. Compared to the rest of the universe, Mars is not very far away from Earth. Since there is plenty of life on Earth, people thought there could be life on Mars too. Even today, people are still trying to figure out if there is life of any kind on Mars.

Why Explore?

Mars is so far away and hard to get to—so why should we bother exploring it at all? There are a few answers to that question.

First, Mars is the closest place to look for life. Humans are very curious about whether Earth has the only life in the universe. If we can find life on Mars, we'll know more about life in general.

Scientists want to know if there is water on Mars. If we can find water, then we might be able to find life too. Scientists have found *evidence* that water at least used to exist on Mars! But for a long time, they weren't sure if it was still there.

Mars is a good place to learn about other things as well. For example, there is evidence that Mars' climate has changed. Now, the Earth is facing climate change too. By studying climate change on Mars, we can learn some useful things to use on our planet.

Getting to Mars is also the next step in space exploration

The **surface** of a planet is the ground. It's the outside of the planet.

Craters are pits in the ground caused by a meteorite hitting a planet.

Evidence is information that is used to prove a theory.

because, after the moon, Mars is the next closest major object to the Earth. We already know we can get to the moon. If we get to Mars, we'll have figured out how to travel longer distances in space. And after Mars, we could go even farther.

Human beings have always wanted to explore. They just want to learn more, whether it's about another continent, under the ocean, or a faraway planet. Exploring is part of what makes us human!

Flying By the Red Planet

For a long time, people didn't have enough *technology* to even get close to Mars. All they could do was look at it through telescopes.

But by the middle of the twentieth century, space exploration technology was a lot better. The Soviet Union sent up the first manmade satellite in 1957. Soon after, the first person was launched into space. And by 1969, we were landing people on the moon.

Space exploration had come a long way. A lot of people were paying attention to getting to the moon. But some people were still thinking about Mars too.

In the United States, the organization that explores space is called the National Aeronautics and Space Administration (NASA). In 1964, NASA launched a spacecraft that was set for Mars. The spacecraft was named *Mariner 3*. *Mariner 3* wasn't supposed to

First Telescopes

Telescopes have helped scientists learn a lot about the universe. A man named Hans Lippershey invented the very first telescope in 1608. He made eyeglasses, so he used his invention to help people see better. A year later, the famous astronomer Galileo used Lippershey's idea to build a telescope that could look into the night skies. With his telescope, Galileo discovered that Saturn had rings. He found four of Jupiter's moons. Stars and planets that had been only tiny points of light could now be studied more closely.

In 1961, NASA scientists showed President Kennedy a model of the Mariner *spacecraft they would launch a year later. The* Mariner 1 *spacecraft failed, but* Mariner 2 *managed to get to Venus and* Mariner 4 *made it to Mars.*

land on Mars. All it had to do was fly by the planet.

People had never sent anything so far in space. NASA wasn't sure *Mariner 3* would even get there. And in fact, *Mariner 3* didn't reach Mars. The spacecraft was designed to use **solar power** to travel out in space—but a protective shield covering the spacecraft didn't open the way it was supposed to. All the instruments on board were still under the shield, so they couldn't do their jobs. Sunlight couldn't reach the solar panels on board, so the spacecraft ran out of power.

Just a couple weeks later, however, NASA launched *Mariner 4*. This time, the spacecraft did reach Mars! Everything went smoothly, and it successfully flew by the planet.

The spacecraft took more than seven months to get to the red planet, but it stayed in space for three years. As it flew by Mars, *Mariner 4* took pictures. Until then, no one had known exactly what the surface of Mars looked like. The pictures showed a dry, dusty, and lifeless planet.

Mariner 4 was just the beginning. Scientists had a lot of questions about Mars—and now they could start finding answers.

Solar power is energy that is absorbed from the sun.

Data is information gathered during scientific experiments.

A **mission** is a trip that you take to achieve a certain goal.

To **orbit** means to fly around and around something in space.

Next Steps

Now NASA knew it could reach Mars with a spacecraft. NASA sent two more spacecraft in 1969. *Mariner 6* and *7* both reached Mars. They took even more photos, especially of the planet's equator and south pole.

Mariner 6 and *Mariner 7* also collected a lot of data for scientists back on Earth. They took readings of the atmosphere and surface. Scientists learned that the south pole was covered with a cap of ice made out of carbon dioxide.

So far, everything was going pretty well. NASA had reached Mars with three different missions. They tried again with *Mariner 8*.

Like *Mariner 3*, however, this spacecraft didn't make it. The launch went wrong. The spacecraft didn't even make it to space, much less Mars.

Luckily, *Mariner 9* did successfully reach Mars. This time, it didn't just fly by the planet. *Mariner 9* was another first—the first manmade object to orbit Mars. When it got there, though, Mars was in the middle of a huge dust storm. *Mariner 9* had to wait until the dust storm stopped before it could start taking clear pictures.

Like the other Mariner missions, *Mariner 9* sent back lots of pictures. It mapped most of the planet's surface, and took lots more readings about the atmosphere and surface.

President Johnson takes a look at some of the photos sent back by the Mariner probes. This was the first time in history that we were getting a good idea of what other planets looked like!

Scientists now knew exactly what Mars looked like. They had a map of its volcanoes and craters. They saw what looked like dry rivers and other evidence that there used to be water on Mars. They also had pictures of the two moons, called Phobos and Deimos.

More Orbiters

NASA wasn't done sending orbiters to Mars. In 1996, it sent the *Mars Global Surveyor* up into space. The spacecraft was supposed to orbit Mars and collect even more information. NASA hadn't had an orbiter around Mars in over ten years. It was time for more data.

The *Mars Global Surveyor* did a lot more than it set out to do! It lasted for ten years, much longer than scientists had planned. In those ten years, it took more pictures of the surface. The Mars Orbiter Camera was on board, which took really wide photos. They were much more *detailed* than the photos from the 1960s and '70s.

The *Mars Global Surveyor* also created a weather map of the planet. It took weather measurements every day. Scientists could see that Mars has weather patterns, just like Earth does. Instead of rain though, Mars has dust storms.

The pictures also gave us even more evidence that there was once water on Mars. Patterns on the surface looked like water had moved things around. *Mars Global Surveyor* didn't actually find any water, though.

Finally, in 2006, NASA lost contact with the *Mars Global Surveyor.* Since the spacecraft was only supposed to work for five years, ten years was pretty good, though!

The next Mars orbiter has lasted even longer. The *2001 Mars Odyssey* launched in 2001. As of 2013, it is still orbiting Mars. *Odyssey* holds the record for the longest-lasting spacecraft orbiting a planet.

Like the other orbiters, it has taken lots of photos. It collects lots of data about geology and climate. In 2002, *Odyssey* found even more

Scientists at NASA put the Mars Global Surveyor in its protective canister to make the long trip to Mars.

evidence of water. It showed scientists there was a good chance Mars has a lot of ice near its poles. Maybe some of this ice is made of water, instead of carbon dioxide.

International Orbiters

The United States isn't the only country launching spacecraft. The Soviet Union (which is now Russia) was also very involved with space exploration during the twentieth century. It still is today too.

In the early 1970s, the Soviets sent two orbiters to Mars—*Mars 2* and *3*. *Mars 2* crashed into the surface, but *Mars 3* made it to the planet and started orbiting. *Mars 3* gave Soviet scientists photos and data, adding to people's knowledge of the red planet.

Today, the European Space Agency (ESA) has an orbiter called *Mars Express*. The orbiter has been collecting information since 2004.

Mars Express was sent to look for water. It has equipment that can get information about what is under the planet's surface. Scientists think Mars might have underground water.

An instrument called MARSIS (the Mars Advanced Radar for Subsurface and Ionospheric Sounding) lets *Mars Express* look underground. ESA, the Italian Space Agency, and NASA together built MARSIS. Thanks to MARSIS, *Mars Express* can see things like underground ice and buried craters.

Once frozen water was discovered, the orbiter studied ice at the Martian poles. It also discovered another kind of gas, methane, in the atmosphere.

Altogether, the orbiters launched by the United States and other countries have helped us learn a lot about Mars. But a different kind of spacecraft—the Mars landers—also made discoveries.

Roadblocks

Although people have gotten better at sending spacecraft to Mars, it still doesn't always work out perfectly. In 1992, NASA launched *Mars Observer*, a new satellite meant to orbit Mars. *Mars Observer* had lots of equipment to do more studies about the geology, climate, and atmosphere. Just before it entered Mars' orbit, though, scientists lost contact with the spacecraft. The mission had failed. Later missions gathered the same information Mars Observer was supposed to have collected. Then in 1999, *Mars Climate Orbiter* also didn't reach Mars. It burned up in Mars' atmosphere before it could do its job.

Find Out Even More

Reading books like the one you're holding now is a great way to learn more about your favorite things. Do you like space shuttles and rocket science? Are you interested in missions to the moon or the Hubble telescope? Pick up another book on space exploration or NASA at your local library to learn more about the topics you're curious about. Your school library or a public library should have books about almost any subject you could think of.

You can learn a lot from reading about the topics that interest you, but each book can only hold so much information. The book's author had to pick and choose what to put in the book and what to leave out. No one book can hold all the information you'd ever want to know about a subject. To get a fuller picture of the things you're reading about, it's a good idea to pick up more than one book on the same topic.

Check your school or public library for some of the books listed below. If you can't find these titles in the library's catalog, ask a librarian for help. If you're still having trouble, try searching for other books about the same topic.

Rusch, Elizabeth. *The Mighty Mars Rovers: The Incredible Adventures of Spirit and Opportunity (Scientists in the Field Series)*. New York: Houghton Mifflin Books for Children, 2012.

Carson, Mary Kay. *Far-Out Guide to Mars (Far-Out Guide to the Solar System)*. Berkeley Heights, N.J.: Bailey Books, 2010.

Siy, Alexandra. *Cars on Mars: Roving the Red Planet*. Watertown, Mass.: Charlesbridge Pub Inc., 2011.

Look over the pages of the book. Check out the table of contents near the beginning of the book. After looking at the book and leafing through some of its pages, ask yourself a few questions:

1. How is the information in the book organized? Do you think it would be easy to find what you're looking for using the table of contents or index (at the back of the book)?
2. Is there information in this book that you didn't find in another book? What did you learn from this book that you didn't learn from the other?
3. Does the book have photos or other pictures? How do they help you understand the book's subject?
4. Do you have any trouble understanding the book? Are there a lot of words you don't understand? Not every book is the same. Some are written for older readers, some for younger. Some books are written for new readers and some are written for people who have been reading for years and years. Make sure to look for books that match your reading level. You don't want a book that's too easy to read or a book that's too difficult to understand. Push yourself, but make sure you're not in over your head and missing the information in a book that's tough to read.
5. Would you want to read the whole book? Why or why not? Is there a part of the book you'd want to read more than others? What draws you to that part of the book?

TWO

The First Landers

Mars obiters circled around the planet. They never landed. Orbiters were the first step in getting to Mars, and they gave scientists a lot of information. But they were thousands of feet above Mars' surface. They could only do so much.

Scientists wanted a closer look. They wanted to see exactly what the surface looked like from the ground, instead of looking down at it from miles above. They wanted to figure out exactly what was underground. Searching for water was hard from up in the air too. If scientists could get down lower, they could look for more proof that Mars has water. And then maybe they could find evidence of life.

Mars landers actually reached the surface. They landed and then moved around, collecting scientific information.

Several landers have reached Mars. They have done detailed experiments and made amazing discoveries. Landers are the next-best things to putting humans on Mars.

The Viking 1 *mission lifts off from Cape Canaveral. The* Viking 1 *rover kept sending back information for more than six years!*

More Details

Landers put manmade objects right on the surface of Mars. They had arms to pick up rocks. They had equipment to do experiments. They had instruments to measure wind and dust right on the ground.

NASA has launched several landers, starting in the 1970s. Each one has taught us more and more about Mars.

Viking Missions

In 1976, NASA flew two *Viking* missions to Mars. Before, all the Mars missions had been orbiters. Now NASA had enough technology to land a spacecraft.

Each *Viking* mission had two parts. One was an orbiter, and one was a lander. The whole spacecraft would fly to Mars. Then it would separate, and half would go down to the surface.

Like the orbiters, the *Viking* landers took photos. They collected data. But they were right on Mars! They could do experiments and get information that orbiters couldn't.

The *Viking* landers did some experiments to test for life. They didn't find any life, but the experiments were interesting. Robotic arms scooped up dirt. Then special equipment on the landers tested the dirt for organic compounds, tiny molecules that have the element carbon in them. All life is made up of organic compounds. If scientists could find some, life might be nearby.

At the time, scientists thought *Viking* didn't end up finding any organic compounds. But thirty years later, other scientists took another look at the experiments.

They realized that *Viking* really had found organic compounds! The scientists just didn't realize it. With new technology and knowledge, the scientists today could tell that *Viking* had found those compounds.

A Mars Mystery

One of the landers NASA tried to launch was called the *Polar Lander*. It was meant to land near Mars' south pole, near the ice cap. *Polar Lander* would study the weather and climate with lots of high-tech instruments. But when it landed, NASA lost contact with the spacecraft. They never heard from it again. No one could figure out what happened. They also couldn't find it. Other Mars spacecraft have taken pictures of the area, but they haven't been able to see what happened to *Polar Lander*.

Engineers always have to think about how their spacecraft are going to land safely on another planet. The Pathfinder spacecraft was surrounded by huge airbags, so it would gently bounce to a stop.

Like some of NASA's other missions, the *Viking* missions ended up lasting longer than planned. *Viking 2* lasted until 1980. *Viking 1* lasted until 1982.

Pathfinder

The *Viking* missions were a huge step forward. But these spacecraft didn't move around once they reached the planet's surface. The landers could only collect data where they sat. They couldn't go to another part of the planet. The *Pathfinder* lander changed all that.

The *Pathfinder* lander was like a shell. It kind of looked like a pyramid. NASA designed the lander to gently touch down on Mars, without damaging anything inside.

Inside the lander was the rover. A rover is a robot that travels over the surface of Mars. The *Sojourner* rover was inside the *Pathfinder* lander.

Pathfinder traveled to Mars, and then dropped through the atmosphere. It had a parachute to slow it down. It also had airbags to help it land softly.

Once it touched down, *Pathfinder* released its rover. *Sojourner* only weighed about twenty pounds. It had six wheels, and a flat top with solar panels. Even though it was small, the rover could do a lot.

Right away, *Sojourner* started exploring. It moved about one centimeter a second. By the end of its mission, it hadn't gone further than a few dozen feet away from the lander. But that was more than any other spacecraft to Mars had ever done before.

Both the lander and the rover took pictures. They did experiments on Martian rocks. They measured the wind. They tracked weather patterns. This was as up close and personal with Mars as scientists had ever gotten!

One of the most exciting discoveries was that Mars may once have been warmer and a lot wetter. *Pathfinder* and *Sojourner* found evidence that liquid water used to exist on the red planet.

Find Out Even More

Reading books at the library can be the best way to get a lot of information quickly. But that's just one way to learn about your favorite subjects. Searching for information on the Internet is another way to find a lot of information about a huge number of topics. There is no limit to the amount of information the Internet can hold, so there's always more to learn!

One of the ways to start looking for information online is to use search engines. Search engines help find the sites on the Internet that best match the words you're searching for. Type almost any key word into the search bar on Google, Yahoo!, or Bing, and you'll find millions of results. Key words are words that help to narrow your search. The more specific your key words are, the better your search results will be.

Try searching for some of the key words below on Google.com. Type any of these key words into the search bar and you'll likely get back millions of results.

European Space Administration (ESA)
Mars
International Space Station
NASA
Opportunity
Curiosity
Mars

Observer
Spirit
ExoMars
Polar Lander
Sojourner

Google searches the Internet to bring you the best websites on the subject you're looking for, but it's up to you to decide which site has information that's important to you. When you pick up a book from the library, the book's author has done the work of putting together information for you. She's done the research and organized the facts. When you're looking up information online, you have to put the facts together yourself. You'll have to work a bit harder, but you'll be learning a lot as you go!

THREE

Advanced Landers

Viking and *Pathfinder* were just the beginning of the Mars lander missions. NASA decided landers worked well. Since NASA still couldn't send an actual person to Mars, the lander and rover were great explorers. More landers followed the first ones.

Two Explorers

In 2004, two landers touched down within three weeks of each other. They landed on opposite sides of the planet. Inside were two more rovers set to explore Mars.

The first rover was called *Spirit*. The second was called *Opportunity*. Their names made people think of hope and adventures. Both were supposed to work for 90 sols, which are Martian days. One Martian day is just a little longer than an Earth day—so they were supposed to last for about three months.

Using the various spacecraft that have been sent to Mars, NASA has been able to perform tests on the soil at many different places on the surface of Mars.

Like *Sojourner*, the rovers had six wheels and a solar panel. They were a lot bigger than *Sojourner*, though. Each was five feet high, seven and a half feet wide, and five feet long. On top was a camera on a pole. With all their equipment, the rovers were heavy; they each weighed 400 pounds.

Meteorites are small rocks from space that hit a planet's surface.

Clay is made up of very, very small pieces of rock that are usually formed by water erosion.

The two rovers continued the work that the orbiters and first landers had done. Their main goal was to find evidence of water. Each sent a lot of useful information back to Earth. Scientists discovered things they had never known before. One of the rovers filmed dust devils, like little tornadoes. The rovers photographed clouds, which hadn't been seen before on Mars. They found **meteorites** on the surface. And the rovers did their main job—they found evidence of water!

This evidence wasn't a lake or a stream, though. It was a kind of rock. *Spirit* discovered silica, a material that's also on Earth. It is formed when hot water reacts with rocks. So maybe hot water used to run on Mars, too, to make the silica.

One of the most exciting things *Opportunity* found was some evidence that Mars may once have been able to have life on it. *Opportunity* found **clay**. Clay means that at some point, water was there not just for short period, but for a while, even if it was a long time ago. And that means life might have been able to exist.

Spirit even took a picture of Earth. Our planet is just a tiny dot in the Martian sky. Think how small Mars looks from here. From Mars, Earth looks just as small.

After three months, both rovers were still working fine. They kept on sending information back to Earth. They kept exploring.

However, they did start to wear out. *Spirit* used a rock drill bit so much that the bit wore down and was no longer useful. One of its wheels stopped working. Now, scientists had to make it drive it around backward.

Eventually *Spirit* got stuck on the surface. The scientists on Earth tried to get it unstuck for months. They couldn't do it. Instead, they

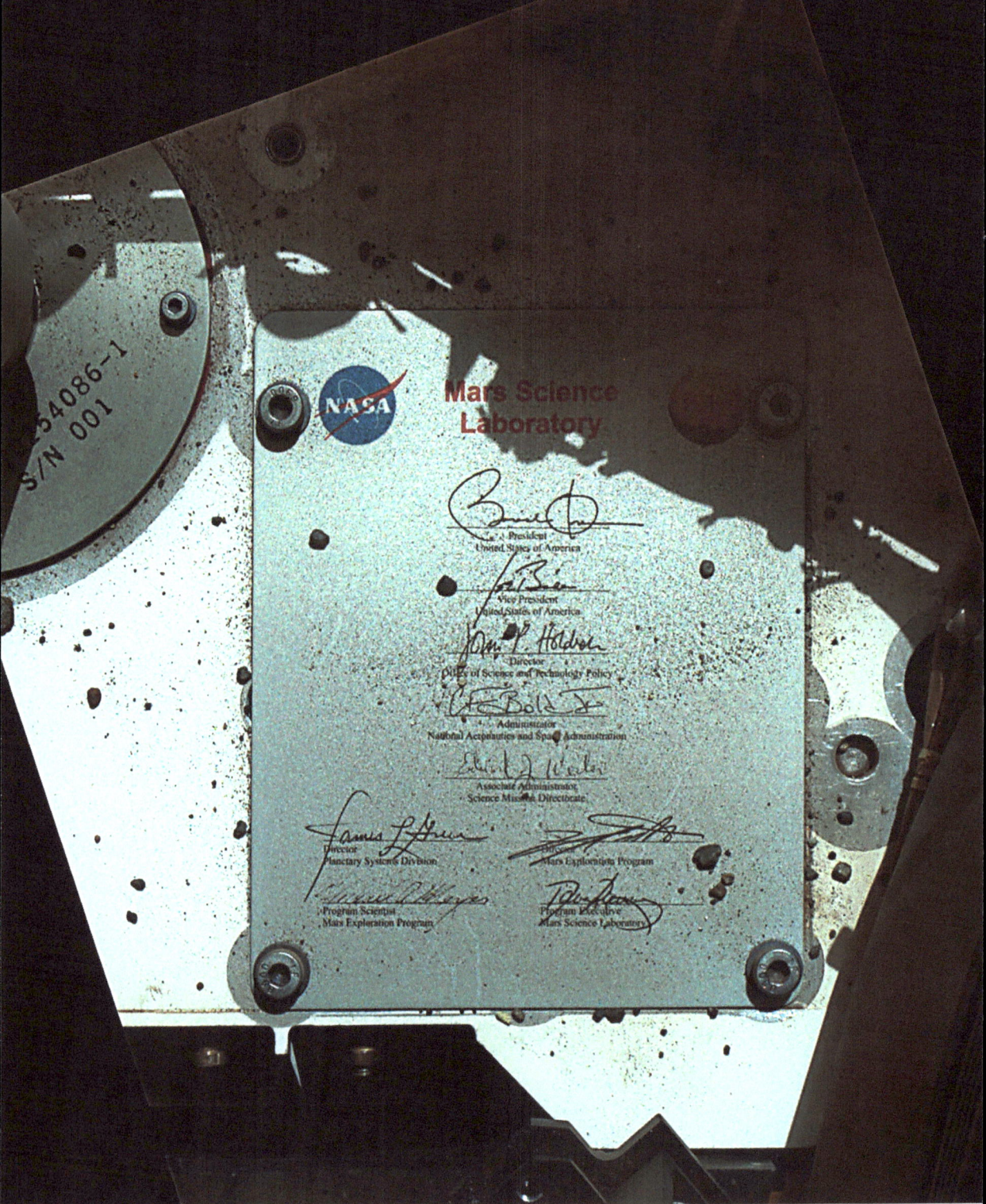

Curiosity has a plaque displaying the signatures of several United States officials, including that of President Barack Obama. Sending a spacecraft to another planet is a very significant undertaking!

**Opportunity Rover
July 8th, 2013**

Opportunity is seen from space as it travels across the Martian surface. The blue color of this region is caused by "blueberries," or tiny chunks of a blackish-blue rock called hematite.

turned *Spirit* into a "stationary research station." *Spirit* could still collect data. It just couldn't roll around anymore. *Spirit* kept working until 2010, when it stopped sending messages to NASA.

Opportunity, on the other hand, kept going—and going. As of 2013, it was still exploring. Scientists are glad for every extra minute they get from the rover!

Water!

Spirit and *Opportunity* weren't the only manmade objects on Mars in the 2000s. In 2007, NASA sent the *Phoenix* lander. This lander didn't have a rover, but it still did important work.

Something that is **stationary** doesn't move.

Research is the work you do to gather data and make new discoveries.

937 to 1013 nm slope x10^{-4} nm^{-1}

The colors in this infrared scan of the surface of Mars show the presence of frozen water. Scientists have long suspected that there was water on Mars, but it wasn't until recently that they were able to find it.

Phoenix's job was to keep looking for water on Mars.

Phoenix landed near the north pole, where a few years before, the *Odyssey* orbiter had shown scientists that they might be able to find water or ice. Phoenix was sent there to get a closer look.

After *Phoenix* landed, it started digging. It dug through the surface and brought up the material under the ground. Just a few inches underground, *Phoenix* found ice!

When the lander brought it up to the surface, the ice sublimated. That means it turned from a solid (ice) to a gas. The ice skipped the liquid water phase because of Mars' thin atmosphere.

Mars has very low air pressure. That means the air doesn't press very hard on the surface of the planet. Low pressure makes water vapor turn right into ice. Ice can do that on Earth too. For example, ice from glaciers can turn right into water vapor, especially when there is low pressure, wind, and lots of sun.

Scientists had found the first actual proof of water! All the orbiters and landers and rovers that had come before had shown scientists there was probably ice around. Now they knew for sure.

Martian Blueberries

One of the strangest things Opportunity has found on Mars are the so-called "blueberries." No, they're not edible—they're round globs of iron oxide. In photos, they look blue. Scientists think that liquid water might have formed the blueberries in the past.

Big Rover

The rovers NASA was building were getting bigger and bigger. NASA's biggest Mars rover project right now is *Curiosity*. This rover is the size of a car!

Curiosity is so big because it has so many scientific instruments onboard. *Curiosity* has a big job. All those instruments continue to do a lot of experiments.

Rovers have come a long way from the very first ones to land on Mars. *Curiosity* can travel 660 feet a day. It can roll over big objects so it won't get stuck like *Spirit* did.

The surface of Mars may look like it's just an empty desert, but we have already found water, and we're hoping to find signs of life one day soon.

Curiosity also proves people can land something big and heavy on Mars. If we ever want to send humans there, they'll have to travel in big, heavy spacecraft. Now we know it's possible.

Curiosity also has a big goal. It's supposed to figure out if Mars could ever support life. Did it ever have an environment where living things could grow? Could it ever have that kind of environment in the future? *Curiosity* might tell us. It's specifically looking for tiny *microbes* that lived in the past.

Science On-Board *Curiosity*

The rover *Curiosity* has a lot of complicated parts on it. The rover is meant to do some very advanced scientific experiments. Here are just a few of its parts:

- Radiation Assessment Detector: measures radiation at the surface. Radiation is a type of energy that travels in waves, like sunshine, microwaves, and x-rays. We need to know how much radiation there is to protect any humans that may eventually go to Mars because some radiation is harmful.
- ChemCam: A laser that can vaporize little bits of materials on the surface. Vaporizing something means turning a solid object into gas. The ChemCam has an instrument that can figure out what was in the material that it vaporized.
- Alpha Particle X-Ray Spectrometer: An instrument that measures the amounts of different chemicals in rocks.
- CheMin: A tool that uses X-rays to measure minerals in rocks collected by the robotic arm.
- Rover Environmental Monitoring System: Like weather equipment on Earth, the system measures the temperature, humidity, air pressure, and winds on Mars. It also measures UV levels (the rays from the sun that cause sunburns).
- Dynamic Albedo of Neutrons: This instrument with a fancy name looks for hydrogen under the ground. Hydrogen could be a sign that water was once there, since water—H_2O—contains hydrogen atoms.

Curiosity has a camera mounted on a robotic arm, which lets it take close-up pictures of rocks and other objects that might be placed at awkward angles.

Curiosity's experiments focus on rocks and soil, and what they're made of. The rover can pick up rocks with its **robotic** arm. It can drill into rocks, and then it can analyze what's in them with the lab equipment it has on board. If it finds anything with the element carbon in it, that's evidence of life! Most living things that we know about have carbon in them. (Though not all things made up of carbon are living.) When scientists found traces of carbon on Mars, that was evidence life might be nearby.

Curiosity has a camera that can take very close-up photos. The camera is called the Mars Hand Lens Imager. Scientists can get a very detailed look at the rocks *Curiosity* picks up with the imager.

NASA decided to land the rover at a place called Gale Crater. The site has lots of clues that water used to be there. And water might mean microbes.

Curiosity has been exploring a mountain inside the crater. The mountain has materials that form only in water. Nearby are some tracks in the ground that show that water may have run there a long time ago.

Curiosity was launched in 2011, and started working in 2012. It's a long way from the Earth to Mars, so it still takes several months to get there. In 2013, *Curiosity* was still going strong!

Something that is **robotic** is a machine that can perform tasks.

To **compete** means to try to win against someone else.

Cooperating Internationally

In the past, one country at a time used to work on space exploration. The United States and the Soviet Union were even in a "space race"! They competed to see who could make it to space first.

First the Soviet Union sent up the first satellite and the first person. Then the United States landed the first person on the moon. They kept trying to beat each other.

Today, though, different countries work together to explore space. The International Space Station is a good example of lots of countries—15 of them!—working together to do research in space.

International Space Station

The International Space Station—or ISS—is a place for people to live in space! Astronauts launch into space, board the ISS, and live there for several months. They do experiments to see if people can live for long periods of time in space. If we ever send people to Mars or beyond, they'll need to be able to survive for years at a time in space, so this is important information. The United States, Russia, the European Union, and Japan together built and care for the ISS.

Curiosity *heads toward Mt. Sharp—you can see the slopes at the bottom of the mountain in the background of this image.*

Curiosity is another good example. The rover has equipment from all over the world. NASA is in charge of *Curiosity* and built a lot of it. But there are instruments from Spain and Russia on board. Scientists from Spain, Russia, Canada, and the United States are in charge of different parts of the rover. Everyone is working together to find out as much as they can about Mars.

Find Out Even More

Picking the right key words can mean the difference between getting the right results and getting information that has nothing to do with what you're hoping to learn about. Because there is no limit to the Internet, some searches can lead to hundreds of millions of results. That's millions and millions of websites that all have information about the subject you're searching for—way too many to go through each of them!

Search engines organize search results in order of importance for this reason. Google, Bing, and other search engines try to list the most important results first. But it's still up to you to pick the best results.

Try searching for "Curiosity." What comes up on the first page of results on Google? You may find some of the following sites:

MSL / NASA
www.nasa.gov/mission_pages/msl/index.htm

Curiosity - Wikipedia, the free encyclopedia
en.wikipedia.org/wiki/Curiosity

Curiosity (rover) - Wikipedia, the free encyclopedia
en.wikipedia.org/wiki/Curiosity_(rover)

Curiosity : Discovery Channel
dsc.discovery.com/tv-shows/curiosity

And there are more than 67 million other results! Focus on the first page to start with. Which results match what you're searching for? Which sites are going to give you information on the Curiosity rover?

The NASA website is probably the best source for information on Curiosity. NASA.gov is the first result and a trustworthy source of information. You can be sure that the information on that site is accurate and up-to-date. The next result, however, might not be what you're looking for. The two results for Wikipedia pages on the list above may look the same, but they don't have the same information. One is for the mission to Mars, the other is the page for the word "curiosity." Which is which? The result from the Discovery Channel also might not be what you're looking for. Curiosity is a television show that has nothing to do with the Mars rover.

Making sure your keywords match just what you want to search for, and then checking the results carefully to pick which sites will be most helpful to you, is all part of finding good information online. It can be more work than picking up a book from the library, but you can learn a lot on the Internet that you can't find in books. Videos, sound, and slideshows are all great ways to get information that can't be found between the covers of a book.

FOUR

Future Missions

From the very first Mars orbiters to today's rovers, these machines have told us a lot about Mars. We have mapped out what the surface of Mars looks like. We figured out what its rocks, dirt, and atmosphere are made from. And we even found water!

Even though we know a lot about Mars, there's a lot we still don't know. We'll keep sending missions to Mars. Maybe someday we'll even send people. The future could hold all sorts of interesting new discoveries.

Bringing Stuff Back, Digging Deeper

Mars landers and rovers are great for studying rocks and soil right on the surface and underground. But what if we could bring those rocks and soil back to Earth?

Bringing things back could be one of the next steps in Mars exploration. Then scientists on Earth could do even more experiments on them.

There's still plenty to learn on Mars—and we'll keep sending rovers and other spacecraft to find out more about the world around us.

Even if we can't bring stuff back, there's more to do right on Mars. So far people have looked at the surface of Mars. Some spacecraft have dug down a few inches or a few feet. We still don't know what's way underground, though. Future equipment could dig a lot deeper.

Digging deep into Mars probably isn't so far off in the future either. NASA is working on the InSight program. The InSight program would send another lander to Mars. The lander would focus on studying what's deep inside the planet. Now that scientists have found water on Mars, they can start looking at other things.

By looking below the surface, InSight could help us understand how Mars formed billions of years ago. We've done the same thing on Earth. But we still don't know everything about how our planet formed. By studying Mars, we can get more information about how both planets formed.

NASA plans on launching InSight in 2016. Then we'll start learning lots of new things about Mars.

Life on Mars

One of the big mysteries has always been whether there was ever life on Mars. Through the years, scientists have found good signs that there could have been life there in the past. Maybe there's even some form of life today. We just haven't found it yet. Even if only tiny microbes can exist there, that would prove that the planet could support life.

2016

You might have noticed that space organizations have a lot of big plans for 2016. They've planned a lot of missions, like an ExoMars mission. That's because in 2016, the Earth and Mars will be close together. Spacecraft won't have to travel quite as far. They'll be able to get to Mars more quickly and start gathering information sooner.

The European Space Agency and Roscosmos (the Russian space program) have come up with new missions. The new missions will look for life on Mars. Together, the missions will be called ExoMars.

ExoMars is scheduled to start in 2016. A spacecraft will fly to Mars and look for methane. Methane is a gas that gives scientists a clue that

The Curiosity spacecraft heads toward the surface of Mars. The landing happened so quickly that everything had to happen automatically—NASA was completely out of control of the craft while this happened.

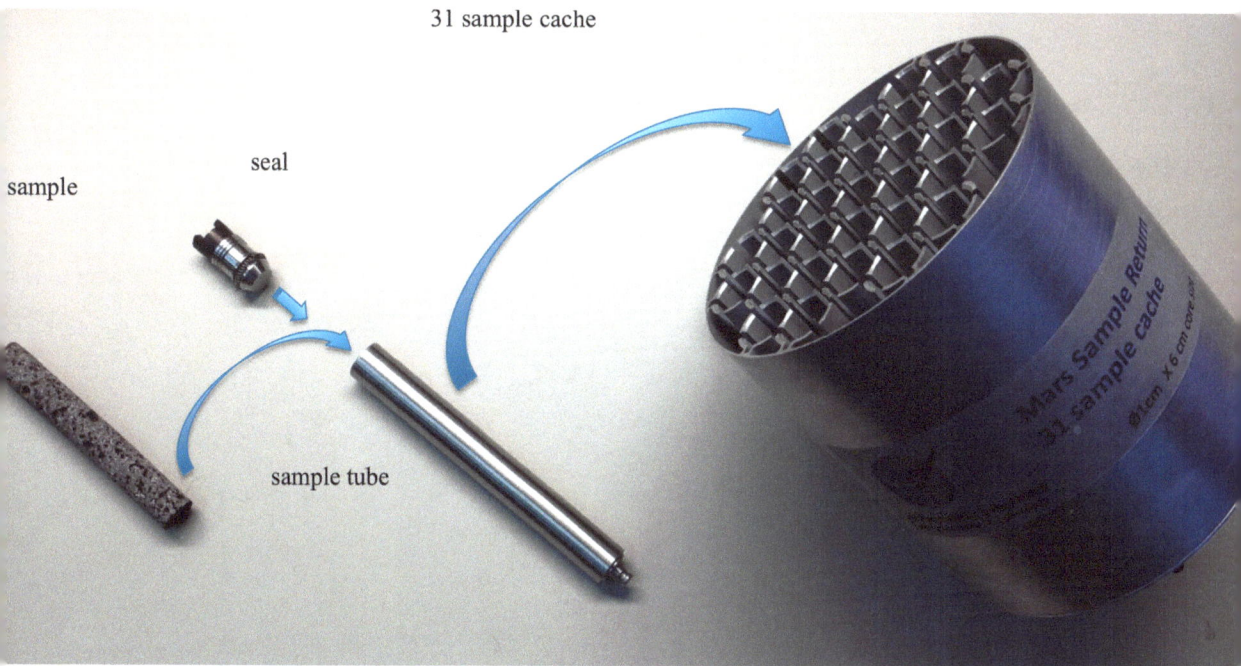

31 sample cache

sample

seal

sample tube

NASA is hoping to one day use a container like this to return samples of rock from Mars to Earth.

life is around. On Earth at least, most methane is produced by living things. Later on, ExoMars will send a lander and rover. ExoMars is sure to find lots of new and interesting data. Maybe it will even find proof of life!

Humans on Mars

Space exploration's biggest goal right now is to land people on Mars. We don't have the technology yet. But we're getting closer.

First, people need to know as much as they can about Mars' environment. They need to be sure they can keep astronauts safe on the red planet.

For example, knowing how much radiation is on the surface of Mars is really important. Radiation is dangerous for humans in high amounts. Because Mars has a lot of radiation from the sun, astronauts would be

SEEKING SIGNS OF PAST LIFE

CONDUCT RIGOROUS IN-SITU SCIENCE

GEOLOGICALLY DIVERSE SITE

COORDINATED, NESTED CONTEXT AND FINE-SCALE MEASUREMENTS

ASTROBIOLOGY

ENABLE THE FUTURE

RETURNABLE CACHE OF SAMPLES

CRITICAL IN-SITU RESOURCE UTILIZATION AND TECHNOLOGY DEMONSTRATIONS REQUIRED FOR FUTURE MARS EXPLORATION

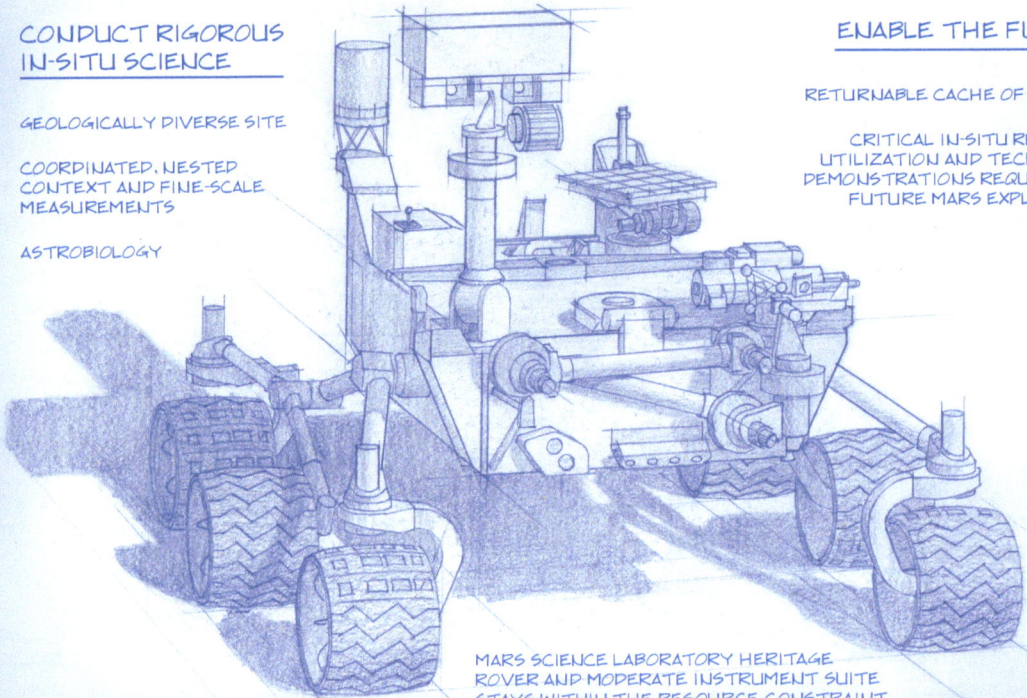

MARS SCIENCE LABORATORY HERITAGE ROVER AND MODERATE INSTRUMENT SUITE STAYS WITHIN THE RESOURCE CONSTRAINT

NASA's plans for future rovers will probably borrow heavily from the design of the Curiosity rover, but with different scientific instruments.

in danger. But engineers could design spacecraft and spacesuits that protect astronauts. Or they could find other solutions.

People would also need to live in space for a long time. Getting to Mars and back would take over a year. Then add in any time spent on Mars. No person has ever gone that far from Earth or been gone so long.

Right now, we're studying how people are able to survive in space. Humans have lived on space stations for months. A few have even lived in space for over a year. Astronauts on space stations have studied how human bodies get used to living in space. They study how astronauts feel about living in space for so long. They are studying how to grow and store food and water in space. All those things are important if humans ever fly to Mars.

NASA has said it wants to get people to Mars by the 2030s! Missions will depend on how much money the government gives NASA. Space exploration costs a lot of money. Each mission is millions of dollars.

But NASA isn't the only group trying to get people to Mars. These days, there are lots of companies involved in space exploration. These aren't government organizations. Instead, individuals have started up companies that build spacecraft. Some companies are working to get people to Mars. NASA gets its money from the government. The people who run companies raise the money themselves. They don't have to do what the government says.

Mars companies have promised some pretty crazy things. A company called Mars One announced it would send humans to Mars by 2018. Another wants to start a Martian colony by 2023. Mars One wants to follow the mission with cameras and create a reality TV show. The company SpaceX is looking into starting a colony of 80,000 people. A seat on a ride to Mars would only cost $500,000!

All those plans sound a little crazy today. But someday they might be normal. After all, flying a spacecraft to Mars sounded crazy a hundred years ago.

We have a lot more work to do before humans can land on Mars. Even though we know a lot about the red planet, Mars is still a mystery. We don't know if liquid water used to exist on the ground. We don't know if there are tiny microbes living somewhere. We don't know how Mars was formed.

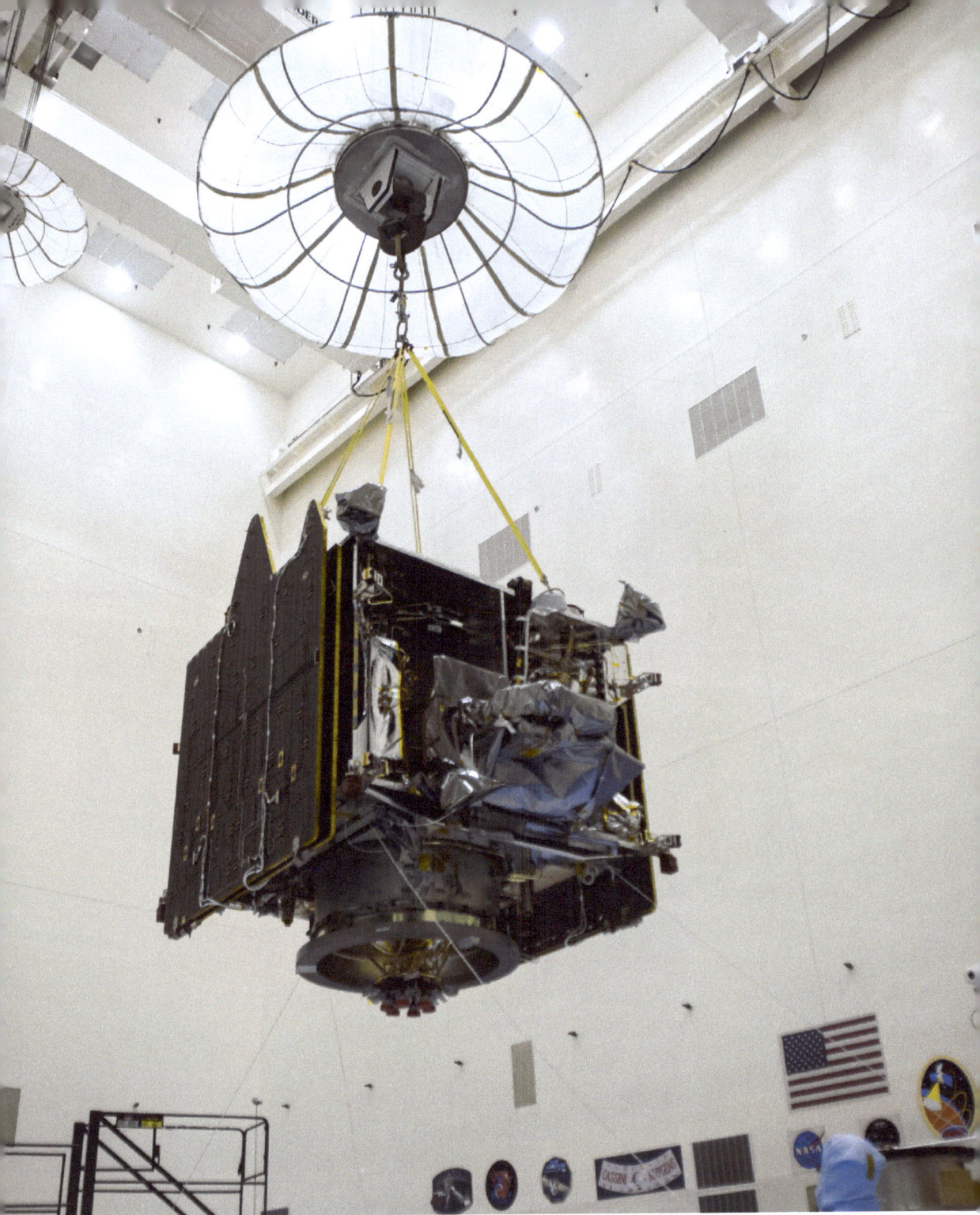

The MAVEN spacecraft is designed to study Mars' upper atmosphere. Scientists know that the environment of Mars didn't always look like it does now. With MAVEN, they're hoping to get a glimpse of what the planet might have looked like many years ago.

We'll answer all these questions and more. More orbiters, landers, and rovers will study Mars. And someday, humans will step foot there and make even more discoveries.

Find Out Even More

Whenever you're looking up information online, it's important to ask yourself a few questions about each site you visit.

1. Who made the site? Is the site run by a government group or a business? Is the site owned by a news organization or is it a personal blog run by one person? Knowing who created the site and who is posting the information you're reading is very important. Everyone has their own point of view, their own way of looking at the world. Knowing what that point of view is can help you decide whether the information on the site is good.

2. Why did they make the site? Different sites are made for different reasons. Knowing why a site was made can help you understand the website's point of view. A business selling a product might have a very different set of facts included than a site that's looking at that product honestly, giving both the good and bad. A news site will likely have more accurate information than a personal blog.

3. How old is the site? Make sure to look for dates on the information you read online. You don't want to read old information that isn't true any longer. You want the latest facts and most up-to-date information. Checking the dates on blog posts, news articles, and other information online is a big part of getting your facts right.

Remember, just because something is on the Internet, that doesn't mean it's true. Some websites are more trustworthy than others. Different websites are made for different reasons, and not all of those reasons are about getting the right information to curious people.

In the same way reading more than one book on a subject gives you a better look at that topic, looking at more than one website is important. If you read something on one site that you can't find on other sites, it may not be information you can trust. Remember to check facts you're not sure of by looking at more than one source.

Here's What We Recommend

If you want to to learn more about missions to Mars and space exploration, here are some good websites and books to get you started!

Online

Expore! Mars Inside and Out
www.lpi.usra.edu/education/explore/mars/resources/websites.shtml

Field Trip to Mars
www.kidscosmos.org/field_trip_to_mars.php

KidsAstronomy.com: Exploring Mars
www.kidsastronomy.com/mars_explorer.htm

NASA: Mars Exploration Program
mars.jpl.nasa.gov

Mars for Kids
athena.cornell.edu/kids

In Books

Oxlade, Chris. *Mars (Astronaut Travel Guides)*. New York: Heinemann-Raintree, 2012.

Rusch, Elizabeth. *The Mighty Mars Rovers*. Mankato, Minn.: Houghton Mifflin, 2012.

Siy, Alexandra. *Cars on Mars: Roving the Red Planet*. Watertown, Mass.: Charlesbridge, 2009.

Index

About the Author

Kim Etingoff lives in Boston, Massachusetts, spending part of her time working on farms. Kim writes educational books for young people on topics including health, science, history, and more.

Picture Credits

www.ingramcontent.com/pod-product-compliance
Lightning Source LLC
Chambersburg PA
CBHW042018080426
42735CB00002B/95